KT-509-984

CONTENTS

Pages 2 - 3
and 34 - 35
Photos by
Dr. Herbert R.
Axelrod

636. 686

Your First
LOVEBIRD

Michael Kelly

© 1991
By T.F.H.
Publications,
Inc., Neptune,
N.J. 07753 USA

•

T.F.H.
Publications,
The Spinney,
Parklands,
Denmead,
Portsmouth
PO7 6AR
England

Introduction

The lovebirds are parrots, members of the family Psittacidae. Other members of this family include the well-known African Grey Parrot, Amazon parrots, and the ever-popular Budgerigar. Members of the parrot family have long attracted and fascinated the human population: it is known that Alexander the Great brought parrots to Europe in the fourth century B.C., and even before this time parrots were kept as companions and studies by other peoples of the world. Yet, despite man's long-held fancy to the parrot family, it was not until the 1800s that man began to keep parrots according to a systematic, research-based plan of accommodation, and thus it was not until this time that parrots were kept by man with any degree of broad-ranging success.

We have come a long way in our keeping of the parrot species. Today it can be assumed that if the keeper begins his undertaking with a sound base of knowledge as to the requirements of his lovebird, selects his first charge from hardy, domestically bred stock, and exercises responsibility and common sense in all his keeping duties, he will enjoy a successful and rewarding hobby.

The intention of this book is to provide such a base for the first-time keeper of lovebirds. Discussed will be the individual species of lovebirds, their general keeping and feeding requirements, and what a responsible owner can expect in terms of taming and breeding his animals. However, before we proceed further, the author would like to add that although lovebirds are commonly kept in the bird hobby—and have been since 1900—and although these birds demonstrate general hardiness and adaptability, it should not be assumed that lovebirds are ideal birds for beginners. Such birds as Zebra Finches and Budgerigars are generally better suited as pets for the first-time bird keeper. By starting the parrot-keeping experience with Budgerigars, novice parrot fanciers gain valuable knowledge and hands-on experience without unduly endangering the welfare of their charges.

Above all, it must be forever kept in mind that we keep birds for the birds' sake, and that all the pleasure we derive from such undertaking is the by-product of such keeping: by keeping the bird's welfare foremost in mind, we to a large degree ensure our success as avian fanciers.

Species

In general, lovebirds, birds of the genus *Agapornis,* are small, stockily built parrots measuring from 5 to 7 inches, with a large bill and a square or round tail; they are typically lively and entertaining birds with good dispositions towards their human caretakers and a demonstrated inclination to breed well in captivity. Of course, there are exceptions to these generalizations. Common to all lovebirds is a base color of green, although many color-marking mutations and permutations exist among the species. All lovebirds are native to the African continent, with the exception of the Grey-headed Lovebird, which is native to the island of Madagascar. For the most part, lovebirds dwell near the Equator; and, with the exception of the forest-dwelling Black-collared Lovebird, lovebirds in the wild prefer dry savannah regions.

Lovebirds demonstrate a strong, close bonding between pairs of the opposite sex—a bond so strong that it is rumored that if one of a pair dies, the other may also pass away from acute mourning. This rumor, however, has not been scientifically verified. Nonetheless, the "loving" bond demonstrated by the species of lovebirds is undeniable. It is not without due reason that the Germans call this bird *unzertrennlichen*; the French, *inseparables*; and we English-speaking peoples, lovebirds.

Yet, lovebirds are not solely "loving" birds. Like us all, they have certain "less desirable" qualities. As a general rule, lovebirds tend to be aggressive towards birds other than their mate, and this quality is especially notable between two birds of the same sex. This aggressive quality holds true to some degree for both conspecifics and lovebirds in the company of birds of other species. It can also be held as a general rule that lovebirds are rather boisterous in their vocal display; in other words, they tend to be noisy, though less so than many of the other parrot species. Therefore, if quietness is a necessary quality in your avian companions, a member of another bird family is strongly recommended.

Yet again, offsetting these possibly negative qualities are the generally agreeable temperaments of the lovebirds towards humans, the entertaining behavior they exhibit, the ease with which many lovebirds breed, the relatively ample availability of several of the lovebird species, and also the indisputably attractive coloration that lovebirds display. So, in the end, if you have determined that the lovebird is your bird, the author congratulates you on a most handsome selection.

Above: Masked Lovebird, *A. p. personata*, keeping watchful eye over its blossoms and greenery. Some owners strive to produce as natural a setting as possible. Photo by T. Tilford. **Facing page:** Pair of Fischer's Lovebirds, *A. p. fischeri*, perched upon a natural tree branch. Masked Lovebirds and Fischer's Lovebirds are both commonly kept in the hobby. Photo by H. Reinhard.

Peach-faced Lovebird: The scientific name for this species is *A. roseicollis*; it includes the two subspecies *A. r. roseicollis* and *A. r. catumbella*. Its native range is the considerably large area of the western coast of southern Africa, where it feeds primarily on seeds, berries, and fruits. Its natural breeding period is between February and March; it is considered a natural colony breeder, breeding together in flocks in the wild. However, it is not necessary to keep these birds communally in order to experience breeding success. In the wild these birds build nests of small twigs and pieces of bark in niches in cliffs and building recesses, and may also breed communally in the nests of weaver birds. Peach-faced Lovebirds are commonly recommended to the first-time lovebird keeper because they are relatively hardy, require little in the way of special care, breed readily in captivity, and are often offered at a reasonable price as domestically bred birds.

Lovebirds with White Orbital Rings: The species *A. personata* includes the four subspecies *A. p. personata* (Masked Lovebird), *A. p. fischeri* (Fischer's Lovebird), *A. p. nigrigenis* (Black-cheeked Lovebird), and *A. p. lilianae* (Nyasa Lovebird). These four races differ in coloration, size, and range but do share common feeding and breeding habits. Their diet is composed primarily of various grass seeds and half-ripe maize; other foods commonly taken include berries,

fruits, grains, and buds. These birds primarily breed in the hollows of trees, but some will also build nests in trees and on buildings, as well as take communal nests of weaver birds. The Masked Lovebird and Fischer's Lovebird are commonly recommended for beginning lovebird enthusiasts. The Nyasa Lovebird, however, is not common in the hobby and has proven somewhat difficult to breed, while the Black-cheeked Lovebird is a rather uncommon bird that is endangered in its native habitat.

Black-winged Lovebird: The species *A. taranta* includes the two subspecies *A. t. taranta* and *A. t. nana*. These birds inhabit high altitudes in their native Ethiopia, sometimes at ranges of one mile above sea level. These birds are not human friendly and are considered by specialists to be among the most "primitive" species of lovebirds. They are certainly not recommended for beginners. These birds feed on seeds, fruits, and berries and are known to enjoy juniper berries and the seeds of particular figs in their native land. Black-winged Lovebirds roost in trees and build their nest of twigs, grasses, and other materials carried to the nest by the females.

Grey-headed Lovebird: The species *A. cana* includes the two subspecies *A. c. cana* and *A. c. ablectanea*. This is the only species of lovebird that is not native to the African continent but primarily inhabits the island of Madagascar. In its native range it favors the open savannah regions and typically avoids civilization. Both races are considered shy birds and, like the Black-winged Lovebird, among the most primitive of the lovebird species. They too are not recommended for beginners. Their primary food is grass seeds, supplemented with grains, rice, and various fruits. These birds naturally nest during November and April. Their nests are built of grasses, leaves, and bark and are constructed in tree cavities.

Black-collared Lovebird: The species *A. swinderniana* includes the three subspecies *A. s. swinderniana*, *A. s. zenkeri*, and *A. s. emini*. As opposed to the other lovebird species, which prefer the dry savannah regions of Africa, Black-collared Lovebirds are native inhabitants of the forest. Their natural diet consists of figs and rice. Black-collared Lovebirds are rarely imported and rarely kept in captivity. They are known to be very fussy eaters in the captive state, with many soon dying of starvation. Additionally, they are very difficult breeders in captivity, due to their natural proclivity to nest in the mounds of termites; the nests are hollowed out by the females. Their natural breeding season typically is the month of July. As can be assumed, Black-collared Lovebirds are certainly not for the beginner.

Red-faced Lovebird: The species *A. pullaria* includes the two subspecies *A. p. pullaria* and *A. p.*

ugandae. Found throughout central Africa, this species has the most extensive range of all the lovebirds. It can be found in either overgrown or semi-open savannah, but typically avoids highland forests. Its feeding habits are similar to most of the other species of lovebirds; feeding primarily on various grass seeds, it also takes berries, fruits and wild figs. The natural breeding season is between October and February. At first glance, it may seem that the Red-faced Lovebird is a good bird for the beginner. However, like the Black-collared Lovebird, it breeds naturally in termite mounds, making its keeping by other than experienced fanciers not recommended. Additionally, the Red-faced Lovebird is not known to be adaptive, and like the Grey-headed and Black-winged Lovebirds, to be among the primitive species of this genus.

SUMMING IT UP

From this overview discussion, it should be clear that there are considerable differences among the various species, with some making good first-time lovebird pets and others being far beyond the abilities of a first-time keeper. Undoubtedly, the best species for the new lovebird owner are Peach-faced Lovebirds, Masked Lovebirds, and Fischer's Lovebirds. For the duration of this book, we will be discussing various aspects of lovebird keeping and care with these three species in mind.

Above: Wild-colored (Green) Masked Lovebirds. This lovebird race has many color mutations, second in number only to the Peach-faced Lovebird. **Facing page:** Pair of Fischer's Lovebirds. There are approximately six color mutations of this lovebird race available in the hobby. Photo courtesy of Vogelpark Walsrode.

Purchase

With the species of lovebird determined, the major owner concerns are basically: Where do I go?, What do I need?, and What do I look for? This chapter will deal with each of these concerns separately.

WHERE DO I GO?

The first concern, namely where do I go?, can be answered simply because we should be dealing with one of the three recommended lovebirds—the Peach-faced, Masked, or Fischer's Lovebirds. These three birds are commonly bred in domestic aviaries, both by commercial establishments and by individual fanciers. To this author's knowledge, the best place to acquire one of these three lovebird species is at a petshop that specializes in birds. The reason for recommending the petshop is twofold: first, the purchaser can be assured a legitimate, domestically bred lovebird because the petshop can offer fanciers a larger variety of color mutations within your chosen lovebird subspecies and second, the petshop will also have most all—if not all—of the bird's required materials. By conducting all of your business with a single proprietor with whom you feel comfortable, you are well on your way to a mutually beneficial relationship—the

proprietor will appreciate your business, and you will soon appreciate the dealer's knowledge and contacts with other bird fanciers.

Other lovebird sources include large commercial breeders and individual breeders. These sources can be utilized by the lovebird fancier, but large commercial breeders may not be in your area, and there is a good chance also that they will not conduct small-scale business with individuals. Individual breeders, on the other hand, may well be in your area, but they certainly cannot offer the selection of a petshop, which likely deals with many breeders, and most individual breeders certainly do not sell the supplies that the petshop does.

In the end, however, the decision of where to purchase the bird is truly left to the bird owner.

WHAT DO I NEED?

The needs of a bird owner include a suitably sized cage or aviary that is equipped with food and water receptacles, perches and other devices; food in the form of seeds, green feed, etc.; sand, grit, and other such substances; a suitable place to locate the cage; and an earnest desire to provide well for the animal. Of course, the cage and its accessories can be purchased at a local petshop, as can the food and grit. In terms of a suitable location and an earnest desire to provide proper care, they are solely within the bounds of the owner and are left to his own educated assessment.

It is very important to be fully prepared before bringing your new lovebird home. This means not only that you have all requisite materials ready in the home but also that you and all the members of the household are fully prepared to assume your new responsibility, especially in consideration of the fact that the lovebird will likely be a member of the family for at least the next seven years. (The oldest recorded age of a lovebird in captivity is 17 years.)

As a final note, the potential bird keeper must consider the possible legal conditions of his ownership. Laws regarding purchase and ownership may vary from country to country, state to state, and even municipality to municipality. If you are a renter, be sure to review your tenant contract and discuss the possibility of owning a bird with your landlord. Otherwise you possibly could end up with an ugly controversy. It is strongly recommended that you purchase only domestically bred birds—for reasons of conservation as well as keeping success. If, however, you choose to purchase an imported bird, if indeed you can find one for sale, realize that serious restrictions and responsibilities will be imposed from various levels of government.

WHAT SHOULD I LOOK FOR?

In discussing what the purchaser should look for when buying his bird, we will go from the general to the specific. Upon first entering the premises of the seller, take a good look around to assess the overall maintenance and cleanliness of the area: it should be immaculate. An unsanitary or otherwise poorly kept area invites disease, and even if the birds themselves appear healthy, they may be carriers or have recently acquired a disease or infection. Of course, never buy the bird or any of its items at an unclean facility.

Your next step is to begin reviewing the seller's general stock. Start by keeping your distance from the cages or aviaries so as not to disturb the birds. In this way you can get a good idea of the general nature and behavior of the stock by observing the actions and interactions of the birds. At this point you are looking for healthy exercise and other activity, zealous feeding, mutual and/or individual grooming, and/or proper sleeping positions, depending of course on the time of day.

Now inspect each of the cages or aviaries individually, carefully assessing the general behavior and appearance of its occupants. Definite warning signs of unhealthy lovebirds include lethargy and apathy, discharge from the eyes or nose, discolored or encrusted feathers around the anus, fluffed plumage, large bald patches and/or skin irritations, labored or noisy breathing,

Above: Pair of Nyasa Lovebirds, *A. p. lilianae*. These birds approach human settlements in the wild but have proven difficult breeders in captivity. Photo courtesy Vogelpark Walsrode. **Facing page:** A hybrid lovebird. The crossbreeding of lovebirds has been going on for years, and one effect has been the reduced availability of pure specimens of some lovebird races. Photo by M. Defreitas.

and sleeping perched on two feet, especially on the ground (birds typically perch high up, on one leg). Not only should you not purchase a bird exhibiting any of these signs but, as a general rule, you should not buy any bird among the entire stock—infection and disease can spread very rapidly among our avian friends. At the same time, check for deformities, especially of the bill and feet. While genetic deformities of a given bird may make purchasing it undesirable, these deformities are not transferred to other birds except through breeding. Overgrown bills and claws on the other hand are typically the result of improper keeping, which should be a strong warning to the potential owner not to purchase any bird on the premises.

Having reached this stage of our inspection, it is time to begin selecting from among the stock for our individual bird(s). Choose a bird that you believe demonstrates the best signs of health and quality. Don't be sentimental and choose a bird that seems "in need of a good home," as you will likely end up with an animal that soon dies. After you have selected a lovebird, ask the proprietor to handle the bird so that you can inspect it up close.

Handling inflicts considerable stress on the animal, and some birds have been known to suffer heart failure as a result of it. Because at this time you don't want this responsibility—and also to better ascertain the seller's expertise in birds—insist that the seller handle

the bird. Once it settles in the seller's control, closely inspect its eyes, feathers, anal vent, and other points already discussed. Additionally, check its breast with your fingers. If the bird lacks substance to its breast, it is likely experiencing some form of nutritional deficiency and is best not purchased. If the bird passes the complete inspection to your satisfaction, you can then make inquiries of the seller regarding the bird and the prospect of its purchase. The objective of your questioning should be to assure the bird's health and proper care, as well as to become aware of any peculiarities that it might have exhibited in terms of feeding, fighting, and/or other behavior.

Now that you have selected your new charge, it's time to close the deal. Insist on some form of written guarantee that allows you to return the animal within a few days if it does not pass the inspection of the veterinarian of your choice. If the bird was imported, insist on all the transport and quarantine papers, or you may find yourself in court.

It is likely that you will choose to keep a pair of lovebirds rather than a single pet. If the seller has already paired his animals, then your job is made considerably easier. In fact, the author recommends that the first-time buyer purchase only "guaranteed" pairs, if indeed a pair is what is desired. It is particularly difficult for novice fanciers to sex birds, especially if the birds are young. Additionally, even if the birds are correctly sexed but have not yet demonstrated compatibility, there is no guarantee that the two animals will coexist peacefully in the confines of the cage. And, if the two birds are of the same sex, there is a very real danger of eventual aggression.

If the new owner desires a breeding pair, the author recommends that he purchase only "proven" pairs, i.e., pairs that have already successfully produced and reared offspring. While "guaranteed" and "proven" pairs will very likely command a higher price than two singly purchased birds, such additional cost is minimal when we consider the likely long-term failure and frustration of otherwise-acquired pairs.

TRANSPORT AND QUARANTINE

Correctly bringing home your new charge proves vital to your successful avian acquisition: the journey home can prove lethal to the bird if the animal is not protected from drafts, panic reactions, and undue stress.

Birds are very intolerant of drafts; and drafty conditions, even if of short duration, can easily lead to illness. Therefore, the transport cage should be fully enclosed, with allowance for ventilation in the form of small offset slits at the top and on the sides of the cage.

Because our parrots will attempt to fly if startled, the cage must be small enough to contain the animal. And lastly, because all the foreign sights and sounds encountered on the way home will stress the lovebird, the transport cage should be made of an opaque material, such as durable plastic.

Additionally, each bird ideally should be given a transport cage of its own. While these transport cages—perhaps better termed "transport boxes"—can be constructed, they are best purchased at a local petshop or bird-supply warehouse. Purchasing a commercial transport cage is the best way for the new bird owner to ensure the safety of his new pet.

If you already keep other birds in your home, you will certainly want to quarantine your new lovebird before allowing it near your existing stock. Quarantine involves isolating the bird for a few weeks in a cage of its own, which allows you to monitor the bird for any developing signs of illness and other undesirable conditions. If your new lovebird is your first bird, then such quarantine is not necessary, of course. You will, however, still want to monitor closely its behavior and condition for the first few weeks. At first sign of an ill condition, contact your veterinarian.

It is important to remember that the first few weeks in the new home are the most critical for the bird. If it is successfully acclimated to its new home during this critical period, owner and bird are likely in for a long, healthy and happy relationship in the context of proper and consistent care.

Above: Lutino Peach-faced Lovebird, *A. roseicollis*. This very attractive color mutation is in part the result of selective breeding. Genetics plays a major role in many lovebird breeding programs. Photo by M. Gilroy. **Facing page:** The Masked Lovebird has proven a rather easy lovebird species to breed; unfortunately, the lack of sexual characteristics has made it difficult to sex. Photo by H. Reinhard.

Keeping

There are basically four different ways of keeping lovebirds in captivity: the cage, the indoor flight, the outdoor aviary, and the freedom method. Each of these methods will be discussed; however, because the vast majority of first-time lovebird keepers will be housing their charges in cages, cages will receive the most coverage. In any consideration of avian housing, such factors as requisite flying space, proper food and water receptacles, safe and effective perches, and other accessories must be explored.

CAGE ACCOMMODATIONS

There are two possible ways to accommodate lovebirds indoors: one is caging them, and the other is keeping them in an indoor flight. From the bird's point of view the indoor flight certainly has advantages over the cage. From the owner's point of view, however, the indoor flight might seem anything but practical.

The indoor cage is by far the most common accommodation for lovebirds. First, the cage should be adequately sized. One undoubted rule stands: the bigger, the better. Wing flapping and stretching, which often indicate the good health and increased well-being of your pet, require plenty of space. Remember,

a large cage is essential for the welfare of your lovebird.

The minimum size necessary for your lovebirds depends upon the number of birds and their relationship to one another. For instance, a mating pair typically requires less space than a pair of individuals, while a single bird will require even less. If you are unsure of the relationship between several lovebirds, then communal cages, with openings between them for easy passage could be ideal. Such cages allow the lovebirds to establish their territories and escape aggression if necessary. In terms of minimum size of single cages, most specialists demand that the cage have dimensions of at least 32 x 20 x 20 inches to house a pair of lovebirds, and 40 x 40 x 40 inches to house several *young* birds. Keeping more than a pair of adult birds in an indoor cage is strongly discouraged. In terms of the desired shape of a cage, a rectangular cage is preferred over a square one of the same area, as the rectangular cage offers your birds more room for flight and other exercise.

After size, examine the construction of the cage. Whether purchased or built, cages must be sturdy, non-toxic, easy to clean and maintain, and offer the birds protection and security. The main frame of the cage, which can be made of wood, metal, or other suitable material, should be free of toxins and other contaminants. Avoid "pressed" or otherwise-treated woods when choosing cage materials. Your lovebird is sure to put its powerful beak to good use on whatever material you choose. Many specialists recommend that the wood and/or metal be coated with a non-toxic lacquer or other finish for cleaning ease. Because you want to be sure of the cleanliness of your lovebird's environment, avoid used cages. If you must use a handed-down cage, be sure to sterilize it with a disinfectant available at your petshop or veterinarian.

It is often suggested that at least two, preferably three, sides of the cage be solid, leaving only the front of the cage to be composed of wire mesh. This will prevent drafts and give the birds increased security in their home. If you opt for an all-wire cage, be sure to locate it in a draft-free, quiet (but not uninhabited!) spot in the home; additionally, including some type of shelter or "hiding" place, such as a nesting box, is encouraged. A bright corner of a frequently occupied room, such as a den or living room, is ideal for lovebirds as long as the temperature is constant and there are no drafts or excessive noises and excitement. The breeze from a constantly opening and closing door may be a hazard to your lovebird, as would be the constantly changing ambient of a kitchen. The tray at the bottom of the cage should be at least one-quarter of an inch high and slide out for easy cleaning.

Lovebirds are avid bathers. Their cages must be equipped with a sizable bathing dish in addition to a receptacle for drinking water. You will also need three food trays, which are best attached to the side of the cage and accessible from the outside.

Selecting natural perches of varying thickness for your lovebird is also important. Plastic perches can be detrimental to your bird's feet and give your lovebird many sleepless nights. By simply providing several natural branches wide enough for your lovebird to wrap its feet one-half to three-quarters around, you give your lovebird comfortable perches on which it can hone its beak and claws and comfortably flex its feet. Just be sure that the branches you use are non-poisonous and have not been treated with any chemicals. Placing the perches at more than one height gives your birds a variety of sitting positions.

Toys are also a nice inclusion in your lovebird's home. Ladders, mirrors and other toys will inspire your bird to exercise its body and mind, and help keep it active when alone in its cage. Many experts recommend putting a nesting perch inside the cage to give your lovebird an added sense of security. This is even more essential if the cage is constructed of wire on all sides.

With the intent of saving money, some keepers are tempted to

Above: Peach-faced Lovebird in flight. One vital component of any plan of accommodation is the allowance for flight. Lovebirds need this exercise to maintain their health and "positive" attitude. Photo by R. & V. Moat. **Facing page:** Keeping pairs is probably the most common way of keeping lovebirds. These two Peach-faced Lovebirds delight their keeper with their characteristically close pair bonding. Photo by M. Gilroy.

construct their lovebird's accommodations. Unless you are a skilled handyman with considerable knowledge of the properties of wood and metal, as well as geometry, what you can make can often be purchased at better quality for less money.

INDOOR AND OUTDOOR FLIGHTS

An indoor flight is an ideal environment for lovebirds. Flights come in many sizes, but experts recommend a size of 6 x 6 x 3 feet as sufficient. Take the same care in choosing a location for your flight as you would a cage to ensure the health of your birds. Drafty rooms are a no-no. The flight should get natural sunlight for much of the day, direct sunlight for part of it, and be dark during nighttime—guarding, of course, against excessive temperatures, and especially excessive temperature fluctuations which can be caused by the rays of the sun. Artificial lights should be used to brighten up a dreary day. Unlike in a cage environment, more than one pair of birds can be kept in one flight as long as they are acclimated to each other. Nesting boxes are more necessary in a flight than a cage, especially if more than one pair of birds is sharing the space. The large size of the flight will give your lovebirds considerable freedom of movement and can, to some degree, simulate their natural environment.

An outdoor flight, widely considered the best way to house parrots, is seldom a possibility for first-time bird owners. The immense cost, not to mention time and effort if the cage is to be hand-made, required to build the flight often prove prohibitive, as may the absence of a suitable climate out-of-doors. However, if possible, an outdoor flight most often best serves the needs of your lovebirds: your birds will get the benefits of free flight and exposure to sunlight, and you will spend less time cleaning cages. There are many good books that can help you construct and care for an outdoor flight.

Our final way of accommodating our lovebirds is the so-called freedom method. It involves giving the birds complete freedom to come and go from the home as they please. Allowing your lovebirds such freedom is a difficult and often very risky undertaking. Freedom-keeping is best left to the experts. It is mentioned here solely for the purpose of information.

SUMMARY

An indoor or outdoor flight is by far the ideal method of keeping lovebirds. However, space will limit most owners to keeping their lovebirds in cages. Having the proper cage for your lovebird is therefore essential to the healthy development of your pet. Most lovebirds fare remarkably well in an adequately sized cage, provided of course that it contains the proper accessories and receives the required care.

Feeding

The importance of proper diet and nutrition cannot be understated. How well you feed your lovebird will contribute significantly to its day-to-day health and well-being and its long-term life expectancy. Of course, proper feeding contributes most only in the context of proper care in all other aspects of lovebird keeping.

It should be clear that the key to proper feeding involves providing your lovebirds with the most varied diet possible: in the wild, lovebirds are free to select from a broad-ranging assortment of seeds, greens, insects and other foods, and thus can adjust their diet in accordance with their instincts and their needs. As your lovebird's keeper, it is your responsibility to replicate this selection as best you can. Presented here is a rough feeding strategy commonly employed by lovebird keepers.

It begins with a standard seed mixture, which typically includes about ten parts canary seed, three parts brown millet, two parts sunflower seed, one part mixed grass seed, and one-half part hemp seed. Some experts assert that these seeds should be offered in separate containers, perhaps in one of the multi-sectioned food receptacles commonly sold in petshops. Offering the seeds separately in this fashion requires, of course, that the seeds be purchased separately. The argument in favor of offering the seeds separately is based on the fact that in so doing the keeper can better assess his birds' intake of each of the various seeds, and thus to some degree guard against a one-sided intake of only a few seed types.

In the end, however, it can be safely assumed that the majority of lovebird keepers feed their birds a standard commercially prepared mixture specially designed for lovebirds. Provided that the seed dish is checked and refilled daily, after all empty shells are carefully blown from the receptacle, a commercially prepared seed mixture proves sufficient for meeting the birds' seed needs. However, one rule stands firm: no matter how the seeds are presented, they must be supplemented with fruit and greenfood, tree branches, and occasional soft foods.

In addition to seeds, fresh vegetables (greenfood) and/or fruits are offered on a daily basis. Ideally these foods are offered variously, perhaps on a sort of rotation basis in which different fruits and vegetables are presented on different days. We begin our discussion of this type of food with sprouted seeds. Every lovebird should have sprouted seeds offered to it on a regular basis. Sprouted seeds are easily prepared following this recipe: submerge the desired amount of seeds (individual or part of your standard mixture) in clean water for 24 hours; rinse the seeds and place them on screening (to allow good ventilation) in a warm location for 24–48 hours; when the seeds sprout, rinse them again and feed them to your lovebirds. An important note: seeds that do not sprout in three days are not fresh, and the entire batch should be discarded. Sprouting a sample of seeds is a very common and simple method of testing the freshness of seeds.

In addition to sprouted seeds, commonly offered vegetables include young lettuce, Brussels sprouts, cabbage, spinach, parsley, as well as dandelion, chickweed, shepherd's purse and others. Some common fruits include figs, soaked raisins, apples, sweet oranges, and soft pears and peaches. An excellent food for our lovebirds is half-ripe maize, still on the cob. Maize is offered fresh only in late summer, but it can easily be frozen for use throughout the winter and early spring. Berries, such as rosehips and rowan berries, should be offered occasionally. While fruits and vegetables should be offered daily, they must be offered in moderation: an excess of these types of foods can lead to digestive irregularities, first evidenced in either loose stools or constipation.

Fresh tree branches, especially branches from fruit trees, provide a very important constituent of the lovebird's diet. In addition to serving as perches and providing the birds with an excellent material on which to work their beaks, fresh tree branches provide our charges with many necessary vitamins and minerals from their bark, as well as roughage that aids in digestion. Fresh tree branches should always be available to the birds and should be replaced about monthly or whenever they are stripped of their bark.

Soft foods, such as hard-boiled egg yolk, cooked wheat and other cereals, are offered but only sparingly, perhaps on a monthly basis and more frequently during the breeding season. As with fruits and vegetables, an excess of soft foods can lead to digestive irregularities.

WATER

Fresh water must be provided on a daily basis. The water should be placed in a container that allows the lovebird easy access: remember that the lovebird drinks by submerging its lower bill and then lapping up the water with its rapidly pulsating tongue. The water vessel should be placed in a shady location in the cage, and it should be washed clean regularly. Another fact for the lovebird keeper to keep in mind is that, while a lovebird typically refuses to bathe in dirty water, the lovebird may freely drink it, and the ingestion of stale water can easily lead to intestinal infections.

A lone Fischer's Lovebird kept free in the open spaces of its caretaker's backyard. The freedom method of keeping assumes certain risks but does have advantages, provided that the terrain is safe and the environment is suitable. Photo by T. Tilford.

Behavior

Many people who choose to keep birds do so out of the desire to have a tame avian companion. Many others, of course, keep birds for breeding, research, esthetics, and many other reasons. If you are one of those people who desire a tame companion, it is best that you select your lovebird from young stock. As a general rule, lovebirds that possess a black coloration to their beak are young birds. Additionally, you might also want to keep your lovebird singly and not as one of a pair, for single birds are typically known to become more tame than those kept otherwise.

After selecting a young bird, the next step towards attaining a tame lovebird involves spending plenty of time with the animal on a daily basis. After the first few days in the new home (once the bird is acclimated), begin the taming process by talking softly to the bird; you should do this while you present its food and water or do your regular servicing of the cage, and at other times throughout the day. Keep your movements slow and smooth—avoid sudden jerks and other motions that will startle and intimidate the young bird.

Once you feel that your companion is comfortable with you, and you with it, you are ready to take the initial step towards hand-taming, which involves gently placing a dowel against the breast of the bird in an attempt to get it to step up onto the dowel. This may well take many tries, especially with older birds, but you can attempt to encourage your charge with sunflower seeds, millet spray, or other treats.

After your lovebird will step onto the dowel, it's time to attempt to have it step onto your finger, which may follow something like this: have the bird step onto the dowel; wait a moment while talking sweetly to the animal and slowly moving your finger to its breast; now try to coax the bird gently to step up to your finger, which, like the initial dowel-taming exercise, may take many tries. Once finger-tame, your lovebird may well be on its way to becoming a very tame companion. Don't expect too much, however, and appreciate any and all affection and taming cooperation that are given by the bird. Keep in mind that birds, like humans, possess a degree of individuality, and there is no guarantee that any given lovebird will attain a predetermined degree of tameness, despite the best intentions and efforts of the best trainer.

Although lovebirds are not considered good talkers—at best they may come to know a few words and noises—they can be taught to perform many tricks, such as climbing ladders and ringing bells. Lovebird keepers who wish to know more about taming and training their lovebirds are encouraged to investigate the available literature.

Essentially, taming involves conditioning the bird to accept and trust you. In so doing, you are building a relationship with the animal that the animal may well come to depend upon. If you are planning on purchasing a young bird, taming it, and keeping it singly, you are assuming very considerable responsibility. We know that most lovebirds are very bonding animals, and without an avian mate the lovebird may well select its human caretaker and trainer as its lifelong counterpart. When this occurs, it is imperative that the keeper provide regular hours on a daily basis to his lovebird. Should he fail to do so, the lovebird will suffer stress and likely succumb to illness.

BREEDING

While the author is certain that a majority of the lovebird keepers who read this book will consider breeding—and likely even at least experiment with breeding—the author is also certain that breeding is best left to the seasoned keepers of these birds. Despite the fact that the common species of lovebirds breed relatively well in captivity and are for the most part hardy and easy-care animals, breeding places considerable demands on both birds

and birdkeeper. Essentially, it is recommended that the first-time keeper not include breeding as part of his first-year plans. Rather, the first-time owner should strive to acquire as solid a base as possible regarding lovebirds, his particular species of lovebird, and indeed his own animals, before planning a breeding.

The keeper who decides to breed his animals must consider the need for a special diet; special accommodations; the possibility of egg binding and other breeding complications, including the need to hand-rear the nestlings; the proper way to conduct nest checks and keep accurate breeding records; likely veterinary costs; and many other factors too numerous to list here. Most important, from the point of view of this book, is that the new owner has a general idea about the demands placed on a breeder.

ILLNESS

Although, once acclimated, lovebirds are relatively hardy birds, they, like all other animals, are subject to various diseases and ill conditions. As is the case with other pets, the key to keeping your lovebirds healthy is prevention. Prevention in the case of lovebirds begins with the selection of an appropriate site for the cage, a site that is warm, clean, and draft-free. Prevention includes the selection of an appropriately sized and constructed cage. Prevention includes proper feeding and daily

Above: A very young captive-bred lovebird. Breeding lovebirds can be successfully accomplished provided that the keeper has acquired considerable knowledge and experience with his charges. Photo by M. Gilroy. **Facing page:** Masked Lovebird in the proper grasp of its owner. Handling inflicts stress on the bird, but proper hand-taming can minimize this stress. Photo by V. Serbin.

inspection of the birds for any signs of illness or poor condition.

Part of the difficulty in treating illnesses in birds is that there are few really distinguishing signs though there are many general symptoms that suggest any of a number of diseases or conditions. Common tell-tale signs of illness in your bird include: watery and/or dull eyes, runny nose, odd breathing of any type, apathy, lethargy, dull plumage, bald patches, refusal to eat and/or drink, and perching at night on two feet, especially on the ground. These signs are a few of those more commonly observed. By far the best method of detecting something askew in your charge is to know your animal well through daily inspections; then, when change occurs, you will be quick to detect it.

Diseases and illnesses can be caused by genetic, environmental (including feeding), bacterial, viral, or other factors. This is not the place to detail all of the many parrot and other bird diseases known, but it is important to make note of "parrot fever," also known as psittacosis. At one time this disease ran rampant throughout the domestic stocks of parrots throughout Europe and other parts of the world. It brought panic, import and export restrictions, and an increased need for quarantine of new birds. Today there is antibiotic treatment for the disease, which must be prescribed by a veterinarian. Because the disease is highly contagious and not limited to parrots—it can indeed infect man—

any outbreak of the disease must be immediately reported to the appropriate authorities.

Parasites often plague our pets, and parrots are no exception. Parasites that occur externally are called ectoparasites and include red mites, mange mites, and lice. If these blood-sucking parasites occur in large enough numbers, they can seriously weaken or even kill the animal. Additionally, these parasites can carry various diseases. In addition to inspecting your animals, it is vital that you maintain the utmost in cleanliness and hygiene, and routinely treat the bird's living area with a proven-safe pesticide made specifically for birds. Common signs of external parasites include bald patches, irritated skin, and scratching.

Parasites that occur internally are termed endoparasites and primarily include various worm forms, including roundworms, threadworms, and cecal worms. Although endoparasites can be signaled by general weakness, weight loss, and loose stools, it is best to have stool examinations performed routinely by a veterinarian, who can then prescribe any necessary treatment.

Feather plucking is a rather common vice in the parrot world; it refers to a rather undefined condition in which the bird plucks the feathers off its own body—and possibly also those of its mate. Possible causes of feather plucking include: nutritional deficiency, stress, poor environmental conditions, disease, and even boredom (especially in the context of a lost mate or companion). Unless the case is mild and you believe that you know the cause and can treat it, it is best to have a veterinarian or bird specialist take a look at your animal. Treatment will depend on the cause of the condition.

Molting is not an illness but a natural process by which the plumage is renewed. During the molt, the keeper must keep watch that no irregularities occur, such as gaps in the plumage or the inability to fly. In general, molting proceeds smoothly, provided that the bird is in fine condition at the beginning and throughout the process. It doesn't hurt and may often be a good idea to supplement the diet with vitamin and mineral supplements and/or sprouted seeds and fresh fruits and vegetables to ensure nutritional soundness at this time.

With the requisite knowledge and responsibility, the lovebird keeper today can be assured of a rewarding hobby.

Bibliography

THE WORLD OF LOVEBIRDS
By J. Brockmann and W. Lantermann
ISBN 0-86622-927-2
H-1092
Audience: Every known color variety of the various lovebird species is given coverage in this masterfully detailed text, with special attention paid to the methods of breeding them successfully.
Hardcover, 6 x 9", 192 pages,
71 full-color photos.

HANDBOOK OF LOVEBIRDS
By Horst Bielfeld
with a special section on
Diseases of Parrots
By Dr. Manfred Heidenreich
ISBN 0-87666-820-1
TFH H-1040
Audience: For the aviculturist specializing in lovebirds and owners of parrots of any size. Of interest to novice bird-keepers as well as advanced fanciers.
Hardcover, 8½ x 11", 111 pages,
117 full-color photos, 10 b/w photos.

BREEDING LOVEBIRDS
By Tony Silva and Barbara Kotlar
ISBN 0-86622-722-9
KW-125
Illustrated with full-color and black and white photos, hardcover, 5½ x 8", 96 pages.

TAMING AND TRAINING LOVEBIRDS
By Risa Teitler
ISBN 0-86622-986-8
KW-038
Hardcover, 5½ x 8", completely illustrated with full-color photos and drawings. 128 pages.